PARENTING AND PRIVILEGE:
Raising Children in an Affluent Society

To Aidan,

Very best wishes,

Mark Harold.

About the Author

DR MARK HARROLD is a clinical psychologist who has practised in Ireland for the past fourteen years. A graduate of UCD, he subsequently earned one of two Masters degrees in the area of Behaviour Analysis and Therapy from Southern Illinois University, Carbondale, USA. He gained his PhD from the California School of Professional Psychology, Los Angeles, where he studied effective approaches to dealing with behaviour problems experienced by families of children with special needs.

Dr Harrold has guest lectured at both Trinity College and University College Dublin on the topic of behaviour management. He has published his research on parenting in international journals and has presented his research and training programmes all over the world, including Great Britain, the United States and Australia.

Dr Harrold is a former columnist with *The Irish Times*, where he wrote about effective parenting strategies. He has made numerous contributions to both print and broadcast media on topics related to behavioural psychology.

Parenting and Privilege

Raising Children in an Affluent Society

DR MARK HARROLD

BLACKHALL
Publishing

This book was typeset by
ASHFIELD PRESS PUBLISHING SERVICES
for
BLACKHALL PUBLISHING
33 Carysfort Avenue
Blackrock
Co. Dublin
Ireland

e-mail: info@blackhallpublishing.com
www.blackhallpublishing.com

ISBN: 1 842180 81 9

A catalogue record for this book is available from the British Library.

Printed in Ireland by
ColourBooks Ltd

Contents

Acknowledgements

Sincere thanks to Mark Cunningham, Kevin Quinn, Judy Nally, Dara O'Donnell and to Ken Smyth and Hugh McGroddy for their valuable advice.

And finally, to my wife, Carol: thank you for being the person who makes everything possible for me.

A word from the sponsors

We all know that the changes we have seen in Irish family life have been seismic in the past decade. Some, perhaps most, of the changes are very welcome, but many of the advantages of an increasingly affluent society come at a price. Most notably, increased affluence and busy lives have changed the way our children are raised.

Some amongst the wealthiest of the leaders in our society have commented to me in recent years that the children of the "Tiger economy" will need to be more carefully nurtured if we are to preserve much of the values we continue to hold dear as a society.

For that reason we turned to an expert in the field, Dr Mark Harrold, to provide a short book outlining his views on this subject. Given Mark's expertise and experience in this field I am confident that *Parenting and Privilege* will provide useful insights for parents and grandparents alike and it is our pleasure to sponsor its publication.

Yours sincerely

Mark Cunningham
Managing Director, Bank of Ireland Private Banking

Bank of Ireland
Private Banking

Introduction

Welcome to what I hope will prove to be a useful tool for any parent who is raising children in an affluent environment. There are more wealthy families in Ireland now than at any time in our history. Attitudes and values have also changed. This presents an enormous challenge to parents who are anxious to do the right thing for their children. So what is the right thing to do?

This book starts with a review of the changed circumstances that exist in Ireland, followed by a look at how excessive indulgence can have a detrimental impact on children and on family life. Chapter 3 addresses some questions that many parents ask themselves about their own approaches to parenting. Chapter 4, probably the pivotal chapter in the book, identifies the key parenting principles. Chapter 5 highlights how every child is different, even children who have been raised in exactly the same way.

Chapter 6 deals with the thorny issue of bullying and friendships, a particularly vulnerable area for children from families of significant means. The dreaded teenage years are dealt with in Chapter 7 and the conclusion is that, if managed correctly, this time of change does not have to be the nightmare most parents of pre-adolescents fear. Chapter 8 outlines some ways of helping children to adapt to changed family circumstances caused by separation or divorce. This is never an easy issue to deal with, but is nonetheless a very commonplace aspect of contemporary Irish society.

Chapters 9 and 10 address the issues of distribution of family wealth and the sensitive aspects of inter-generational family business concerns respectively. And finally, the book closes with a retrospective of universal principles that can be applied to both domestic and business environments.

The aim of this book is to provide practical guidelines to parents on how best to interact with their children in the money-rich and time-poor environment that has become the norm for families. It avoids any technical or woolly language and provides a framework upon which readers can build to ensure that they and their children get the most out of family life.

CHAPTER 1

Wealth in an Irish Context

I t is hardly overstating the case to observe that Ireland has undergone greater change in the past twenty years than at any other time in its history. There is more wealth in the country than ever before. Ireland is no longer an emigrant culture and its finest sons and daughters no longer have to depart for foreign shores to earn their living or create significant wealth. It is now possible to be successful in Ireland as a result of a thriving economy and a vibrant, young population. This prosperity did not come about in a vacuum. Changes in attitudes, values and the authoritarian role of certain institutions have released us from our previous embarrassment about wealth and prosperity. The context of this change needs to be recognised in order to understand Ireland's new-found wealth.

The diminished authority of the institutional Church has certainly changed attitudes. For better or worse, this has led to significant changes in family life and, indeed, in how people go about generating wealth. Divorce is now a reality in Ireland, which has huge implications for how we function as a society. The conservative mores of the Church have been displaced to some degree by consumerism, which is largely driven by what appears on the television: children's toys are marketed through cartoons; preteens are manipulated into wearing overly sexualised clothing as modelled by pop-star icons; and teenagers are heavily influenced by MTV, the inventors of which have packaged teenage rebellion and the teens pay for it with their credit cards. In addition, the Internet has allowed all of us access to unlimited information with the unfortunate dangers of exploitation of young people that go with this medium.

Within the family home, the balance of authority also seems to have shifted. Many parents feel increasingly frustrated by their inability to discipline their children. They are bombarded by a constant stream of advice about how to nurture the child's self-esteem. It is now against the law to slap your child. While this is probably a desirable development, many parents are feeling more and more unsure about how to rear their children correctly. They are aware of what they should not be doing, but very little seems to be available about best practice in parenting. With the greater availability of wealth, the tendency is to provide material gratification for no reason other than it is now possible to do just that. This was not the case a generation ago. How many parents ever went to see Santa in Lapland? And yet for decades psychologists have warned about the dangers of over-indulging the child.

The profile of people with wealth in Ireland has shifted. Most obvious is the new generation of young entrepreneurs who have made their fortunes either through the property boom or as a result of shrewd enterprise during the recent period of economic growth. In relation to family matters, perhaps chief among their concerns is what is the right way to raise young children. When does giving them the best possible start turn into spoiling the child?

Then there are those who have achieved prosperity in their forties, the reward of their efforts over the last twenty years, which have seen Ireland develop from a predominantly agricultural economy to the Celtic Tiger economy of the late 1990s. There are teenagers approaching adulthood for whom a day's work may never be a necessity for the rest of their lives as a result of their parents' success. Unfortunately, the lack of purpose that may result from this realisation can be the most devastating of realities for a young person. Parents are undoubtedly aware of these dangers, but there appears to be little information available on handling these issues. This is probably because the phenomenon has never been so widely encountered in Ireland.

Finally, there is the owner of the family business who is approaching retirement. To whom should the business be left? How can conflict between the children be avoided? What is the optimal way to distribute significant family wealth? None of these dilemmas can be dealt with in a generic fashion and each requires detailed consideration on an individual basis.

The debate on whether our new-found prosperity has had a positive impact on family life is ongoing. What is certain, however, is that Irish society has changed beyond recognition in the past twenty years. There are more people of significant means than ever before in Ireland. The wealthy are no longer made up of a small, self-supporting community who all know each other. Social class no longer has any bearing on accumulated wealth. In addition, access to information, family law, cultural stereotypes, values and attitudes have changed in tandem with economic growth and prosperity. Parents are left to ponder whether the values and practices of the previous generation remain relevant. What values and guidelines must today's parents embrace so that they raise their children to realise their full potential? This book has been put together to assist parents in addressing these issues.

CHAPTER 2

Concerns about the Impact of Wealth on Family Life

"How you bring up children is crucial. If they have a sense of responsibility you do not have to worry about how the money will affect them."

DAVID ROCKERFELLER

I f only it were that simple. The issue of how family wealth will affect the lives of their children is a common preoccupation for parents of considerable means in Ireland. The questions they ask include:

- Will our children grow up "normal"?
- How will our wealth affect our child's self-esteem and sense of self-worth?
- Will our child be exploited as a result of our wealth?
- Can I prevent our child turning into a "trust slug"?

As they strive to create a better life for their children, parents worry that the very success of these efforts could actually inhibit their children's sense of self-worth. "Money cannot buy good kids" according to one expert. Indeed, it is suggested that family wealth could even lead to what has been termed "identity dissolution", i.e. when a teenager learns that their financial

4

security is not dependent on their success in building a career. In addition, children of wealthy families may experience difficulty in identifying whether friends like them for who they are or only because they are from a wealthy family. These issues can have a devastating impact on some young people. For parents, it is important to find a balance between requiring children to earn rights and privileges and allowing them to enjoy the benefits of family wealth.

Many parents are concerned that as they accumulate more and more wealth it will ruin the next generation. Indeed, statistics indicate that much of the wealth created in one generation has evaporated by the end of the next. This suggests that inherited wealth is not often used wisely by its beneficiaries. A term gaining recognition in the United States is "affluenza". It refers to a state of slothfulness, selfishness and disconnection from the ordinary things in life in people who have not experienced the hard work that initially created their wealth. Many wealthy parents fear that their children may become demotivated and develop a sense of purposelessness if they do not need to work. Alternatively, children may feel a burden of responsibility to match the achievements of their wealthy parents. This burden can be exacerbated by the parents' own high expectations of their children. Either way, no parent would wish their children to be negatively affected by accumulated wealth.

In an effort to instil a good work ethic in their children, some parents may be overzealous in insisting that their children earn everything that comes their way. The hope is that this will ensure the appropriate respect for the inheritance the children will ultimately control. In the extreme, this can create unnecessary hardship and will not achieve its desired objectives. Indeed, the term "bratlash" has been coined in America to describe children who become dispirited and reject the family's values altogether as a result of this harsh approach. However, a child who grows up in an environment in which everything is provided will be at an even greater disadvantage. The aim for parents should be to instil a responsible and healthy attitude towards wealth. There are no long-winded solutions to this. The simple recipe is time spent with the children.

As far back as 1881, the American tycoon Andrew Carnegie is quoted as saying, "The parent who leaves his son enormous wealth generally deadens the talents and energies of the son and tempts him to lead a less useful life than he otherwise would." He urged parents to leave a way open for children to better themselves. It is reasonable to suggest that there is far greater satisfaction in spending money that one has earned for oneself than that which one is handed. So the objective at all times when raising children should be to prepare them to be able to earn their living in their own right. Children should value the importance of individual endeavour and achievement.

Another aspect to instilling values in children of means is the establishment of a "moral base" within the family. This will be determined by the parents and can include values such as the importance of education, hard work, social awareness and personal characteristics such as humility, generosity and self-confidence. If parents are unsure about the kinds of values they want to instil in their children, now is the time to put some effort into establishing what these are. Many of the core parenting principles contained in this book should provide the framework within which these values can be formed.

Many aspects of a child's environment will influence how they subsequently mature into adulthood. Parents should never lose sight of the fact that they are the biggest single influence on the kind of person that their child will become and they should therefore work at instilling the values they wish their children to possess. If parents do not take the lead in instilling values in their children, these values will ultimately be determined through information picked up in the schoolyard, from their peers or through media influences.

THE IMPORTANCE OF TIME

"The best inheritance a parent can give his children is a few minutes of his time each day."
ORLANDO A. BATTISTA

Many parents in Ireland today are the first generation to enjoy considerable affluence and as such have no blueprint for how best to manage their wealth for the benefit of family life. If parents want to ensure that their children take on the values that made them what they are, their investment needs to be in time, not money. Money will not replace the time a parent spends with a child. If wealth is achieved at the expense of time at home, parents must decide which is more valuable to them: the welfare of their children or the welfare of their bank balance.

There is no better investment in your child than your time – not money or work, but time. This comes through again and again from every reputable source on the issue of instilling parental values in children. Recent studies have shown that parents are spending less and less time with their children. The irony is that, in the rush to secure the future for their children, they could easily be inhibiting it. A distinction must be drawn between providing wealth for your children and providing security for them. For children, the greatest security of all is to know that their parents love them and want to spend time with them. When problems arise in a child's life, some parents feel that the best thing they can do for their children is to spend a lot of money on the best possible professional help. While professional help may sometimes be called for, it is not always the solution. One professional observed that the most effective part of therapy for the wealthy children he was working with was the drive to and from the therapy session with the parent. In trying to ensure a happy life for children, parents should not underestimate the value of the time they spend together.

It is recommended that the weekends become sacrosanct in the achievement of this objective. Parents are role models for their children and much character moulding occurs in the most ordinary moments – parents can exert most influence over their children's values in the course of the routines of family life. Involvement in the child's football team, long walks to nowhere in particular, flaking out on the couch to watch a film together, pottering around the garage or just relaxing together are more valuable to children than parents will ever be able to calculate. These are the times at which children will learn about and absorb parents' values. It might be how they go about coaching a team, the way they bargain for an item at a local market or even reminiscences about how it was in the old days that leave the lasting impression on children. Similarly, if parents are seen to treat people with respect, their children are likely to follow that lead. And it is not unreasonable for parents to educate their children about the importance and value of money at these times. Above all, parents should remember that their values will not be imparted to their children unless they make opportunities for it to happen.

In wealthy families, as in all other families, it is advisable to move away from the emphasis on money in securing a bright future for children. Fulfilment, not affluence, creates happiness. So where do wealthy parents start in helping their children to secure this state of fulfilment? Much has been made of how affluence can destroy children by creating a sense of guilt, powerlessness and embarrassment about the family wealth. The important point is that if children are to grow up with a strong sense of self and at ease with family wealth, they need to have a purpose and a direction. To achieve this, they must have the opportunity to experience both the highs and the lows of life's challenges. If they are protected from these, inevitably they will be less able to cope with the demands life makes when they have to function independently of family. One commentator has suggested that life's lessons are learned in the valleys and not on the mountain tops. We all need to experience the trials and struggles of life. Children who are given the opportunity to experience life have a much greater chance of developing a sense of responsibility, which will enhance the sense of fulfilment so necessary in the formation of a well-rounded personality.

Parents should allow their children opportunities to fail as well as to achieve to prepare them for adulthood. Reward initiative but avoid overcompensating for losses – children must learn to overcome these hurdles. Allow them to stick their toe in the water and decide whether they want to go on from there. Many of the lessons children learn will not be from parents, but they will come back to their parents for reassurance and advice.

In conclusion, concerns parents express about the next generation are legitimate but not insurmountable. There are many well-motivated, mature and happy wealthy heirs. Much tends to be made of those who fail and this news tends to find its way to the tabloid press. Similarly, the stories about out-of-central rich kids that circulate as gossip in social circles tend to exacerbate parents' fears. However, with some clear thinking and effective communication between parent and child, it is eminently possible to plan for a future that is fulfilling, prosperous and lived with a real sense of responsibility by the beneficiary of inherited wealth.

CHAPTER 3

Am I Spoiling my Child?

By now, we are all weary of references to our booming economy. Nevertheless, the fact is that more people have more money than ever before and it seems that much of that disposable income is being spent on the children. Marketing moguls have certainly picked up on this. How else could you explain the amount of money spent on products like Westlife, Yugio, PlayStation and WWE? But it is essential to point out that money will not buy a harmonious household. Those who have been successful in the world of business may well have learned that money talks – and in the world of business, they are probably right. But in the business of raising children, that particular golden rule does not apply: money will not buy parents' time with their children; money will not enhance children's self-esteem; money will not be the source of children's happiness. Parents are that source. Children are not born spoiled, so for parents it is a matter of getting the balance right between providing for their children both materially and emotionally without overdoing it.

The current environment is very different to that in which even the previous generation grew up. The pace of change has been so rapid that parenting practices have not had the chance to keep up with the changed circumstances. As far as parenting advice goes, the pendulum appears to have swung as far on the side of the child as it possibly could go. There was a time when it was perfectly acceptable to say "No" to children. Now it has been suggested that this will damage their self-esteem and inhibit their sense of freedom. For some, the role of the parent appears to be reduced to that of a support act, catering to the whims and fancies of an already over-indulged youngster. Parents earn the money to facilitate these whims and children are not slow in letting their parents know if it is good enough. This state of affairs is exacerbated by threats to call Childline and the aggressive marketing that convinces children that they cannot survive unless they possess the latest "must-have" items. Parents are all too aware of the manufactured hysteria around the availability of these goods at Christmas time. The rush to provide material goods can be further fuelled by parents' guilt that they are not doing the right thing or that they are bad parents. Unfortunately, parenting advice columns and self-help books do little to alleviate this guilt – perpetuating the guilt seems to sell the books.

At the other end of the scales are the hopes and aspirations of all parents who want to do the right thing for their children. However, they are confused between the current child-oriented trend in parenting practice and their own parenting instincts. On top of all these mixed emotions is the limited time that is available to guide the child in the direction parents would like to see them go. This is an extremely difficult balancing act. It is what makes parenting in the new millennium so difficult and so different from previous generations.

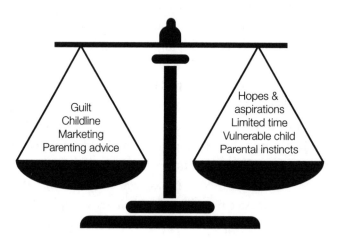

Other aspects of this new era must be recognised as parents develop a strategy to manage their children. Many people would – fairly – say that the "good ol' days" were not necessarily all that good; and who would not wish to improve life for their children? However, it is a question of balance. Children are bombarded with a vast range of influences – including television, magazines and the Internet – which have an effect on their expectations and behaviour. Because of this, their appreciation of the less material aspects of life is dulled and they can be blasé about things that were mere fantasies when their parents were young. For example, a generation ago family holidays – if there were any – were taken in Ireland. Now, it is not uncommon for families to travel to places such as France, Florida or the Bahamas every year.

So how is a parent to get it right in this changed world? There is no doubt that parents today are faced with a different set of pressures than in any previous generation. Despite the availability of endless advice and child-rearing aids, the job of rearing children has become more difficult. Parents are anxious to get the balance right, but are torn in different directions. It is important for parents to realise that ultimately they must set the standard within their household. They know what is best for their children. They must make the determination about how much to give and how much to withhold. Parents should resist the outside pressures that can negatively influence the standards that apply in their home. Children should be encouraged not to be overly influenced by outside agents and to develop independence in how they make choices. One of the original psychotherapists from the turn of the last century, Alfred Adler, was fearful of what he termed the "pampered" child. His ideas are as relevant today as they were one hundred years ago. He expressed concern that the pampered child would not learn to do things for themselves or how to interact with people other than by giving orders. Adler suggested that there could only be one response from society to this type of personality: hatred.

Some parents may feel that material goods help to avoid confrontation with their child; they may find it hard to refuse anything their child asks for in case the child will dislike them; they may fear that if the child gets angry they will not love them. It may come as a relief to many parents to hear that most have been told "I hate you" by their child at some time. Indeed, it is quite normal and not necessarily an indicator of a spoiled child. A spoiled child is one who is self-centred, inconsiderate of others and generally unpleasant to be around. This child sees the world as revolving around them and will do whatever is viewed as necessary to have their own way. Parents may ask themselves if they are raising a spoiled child. Below are some more detailed questions to consider, followed by some steps to take if there are associated concerns.

- **Am I able to say "No" to my child?**
  Children must not be allowed to have their own way at all times, even if it is economically viable to do so. Privileges must be earned. (This issue is dealt with in Chapter 4.) Parents must realise that the child's self-esteem is not going to be destroyed every time they do not get their own way. In this era of obsession about children's self-esteem, some parents find it increasingly difficult to refuse their child's unreasonable requests. It is advisable that they learn how to strike a balance. Otherwise, their children will grow up with unrealistic expectations of the world.

- **Is my child capable of waiting for gratification?**
  Impatience is an undesirable characteristic in children which parents need to address. For example, if a child interrupts an

adult conversation without consideration for those who are speaking, this can be a sign of the child being somewhat spoiled. If the parent interrupts the conversation to respond to the child, the wrong message is being conveyed. The child is learning that they are the only person in the room who counts. Aside from emergencies, it is preferable to let the child know that they must wait until the parent is ready to listen. As a general principle, it is important for children to learn that they cannot always have what they want, when they want it.

- **Do I have household rules and stick to them?**
  Household rules are essential in creating a happy home and, more importantly, in developing appropriate behaviour in children. Children who spend their early years in situations where they are free to do whatever they like or have whatever they want are at a disadvantage when it comes to school, where limits will always be set. And once they leave school, fourteen years later, they will encounter even further limitations on their behaviour. Worse than having no rules is to have household rules and fail to stick to them. This teaches a child that the rules can be flouted.

- **Do I do things for my children for which they should be responsible themselves?**
  My own father used to polish my shoes and repair any punctures on my bicycle. I have to confess that, to date, I have never mastered either of these skills. When the means are available, there is always the temptation for parents to take the easy option and excuse the child from the responsibility. They do so at their peril! It is essential that children learn to take responsibility for their own world, however small it might be at any given time. Let them do it for themselves.

- **Do I give in to avoid the hassle?**

  A friend of mine related that he had no trouble being consistent in refusing his daughter's unreasonable requests for sweets at certain times of the day – but when he was watching a match on television she could have whatever she wanted! Not very advisable, but understandable all the same. It is also understandable that if parents have only a limited amount of time with their children, owing to so many other commitments, the tendency is to give in more often than not. I would encourage parents to try hard to stand firm with established household rules, even if it means that the short amount of "quality time" may be disrupted by a tantrum. In the long run, they will have far fewer hassles and are giving a consistent message to their children.

- **Am I afraid my child will dislike me?**

  Children are very astute at picking up on parents' feelings. This is particularly relevant in an era where practical constraints mean that parents have less time to be around their children. If a parent is feeling guilty for not being good enough or available enough (there are very few parents who do not feel this), children are more than likely to exploit this situation. A guilty conscience is often the trigger to capitulate to a child's unreasonable requests. Too many parenting manuals place the burden of responsibility for the child's happiness squarely at the feet of the parents. The result is that parents can often overcompensate for what they believe the child is missing when they are not there, which can often lead to a child receiving far too much material gratification.

- **Does my child follow through on responsibilities?**

  If there are household chores to be done, it is imperative that the child develops a sense of responsibility around these. It is simply not good enough for children to dismiss them when it suits. Parents can be quite businesslike in how they manage the household rules – there needs to be consistency in applying them and consequences for failing to adhere to them.

- **Do I show my love for my children by buying things for them?**
  It is important for parents to understand that indulgence and instant material gratification are not love. They may temporarily alleviate guilt but that is all they do. If parents find themselves buying items for their children to make up for what they feel guilty about, they must seriously rethink their parenting strategy. They are literally buying trouble.

So much for the searching questions. Below are some suggested guidelines for parents who want to avoid spoiling their children.

- **There is no substitute for time spent with children.**
  Money cannot replace this time. Parents might consider spending money to create more time with their children. This could be done by delegating tasks they normally undertake to professionals specialising in that aspect of their work. It will be money well spent and will help to ensure that their children do not become spoiled.

- **Learn to say "No".**
  Even if children's time with their parents is limited, it is essential that they learn that parents are not simply the suppliers of goodies, but that they give and receive love without conditions. Refusals should not be viewed as withdrawal of love.

- **Be aware that too many advantages can be a disadvantage.**
  Having material wealth creates its own pressures. Unrealistic expectations can develop over time. When the child steps out of the family environment, a very different world may be encountered. Children must learn that it is necessary to earn the privileges that come their way and that they do not have an automatic entitlement to them.

- **It is OK for children to become frustrated at times.**
  This is part of growing up. We all must learn to overcome failure and how to cope when things do not go our way. This lesson must be learned early, as it will be more difficult to acquire as children get older, particularly when children reach the teenage years.

- **Do not buy items for your child just because it seems like a good idea at the time.**
  Save the surprises and special treats for birthdays and Christmas. If a child particularly wants an item such as a new scooter or computer game and there is no special event upcoming, a better idea is to assist them in planning how they will earn enough to purchase the item themselves.

- **Be a parent and not a friend.**
  It is necessary that a clear boundary is established so that the child understands who is in charge. This may not sit well with contemporary parenting advice. However, it creates confusion for children if it is unclear whether the relationship is that of parent or friend. Some negotiation between parent and child is healthy but there must be a cut-off. Too much negotiation will cause problems. In such circumstances, the child will not be able to cope with negotiations that do not go their way.

- **Avoid exaggerated feelings of entitlement.**
  Children who develop a sense of privilege can also develop a sense that they are somehow better than those around them. If this is the case, it must be dealt with directly. They should be shown how to engage with people from all walks of life and taught how to respect all with whom they come into contact, regardless of status.

- **Get children involved in sport and other activities.**
  The playing field is a great leveller. Any exaggerated notions of grandeur can be trimmed very quickly in the field of competition. For younger children, this occurs in the playground. Older children must learn many aspects of getting along with others when playing team games. Scouts, guides, drama and dancing are just some of the many interests that also develop and enhance these qualities.

- **Develop an awareness in children of those who are not as fortunate as themselves.**
  Social conscience is a very necessary attribute for children who are in a privileged position. Some families encourage their children to give their toys to a worthy charity. Others encourage them to donate some of their pocket money for those affected by famine in the third world. By helping those who are less fortunate, children gain a more balanced perspective of the world. Parents can provide no greater experience to their children than one of awareness of social needs.

CHAPTER 4

Guidelines for Effective Parenting

For most people, the only preparation they receive for parenthood is what they remember of their own parents and childhood. However, it is different when it comes to your turn! What follows is a set of guidelines that will put most parents on the right track to effective parenting. Parents who follow these guidelines and still encounter difficulties with their children should seek professional help. The behavioural strategies outlined here are really rules for life and can be applied to most aspects of life, from the home to business. For the moment, however, the focus is on ensuring parents create an optimal environment in the family home.

1. **Work first, then play ALWAYS.**
   Children do what their parents want them to do before doing the activity of their choice. With few exceptions, this must be the order of any negotiation with a child. How many times have parents found themselves saying "You can have it, but only if you promise to be good"? The classic teenage ruse is to borrow money while passionately promising to pay every penny of it back. This rarely happens. It is not a good practice to develop. From an early age, children must understand the importance of earning privileges.

2. **Spend time doing activities of their choosing.**
   This may seem a rather obvious suggestion but it is surprising

how little it happens. It is particularly beneficial for parents who only have a limited amount of time to spend with the children. If a child is secure in the knowledge that there is a time set aside especially for them, parents are less likely to feel constant demands on their time and the child is less likely to feel ignored or overlooked in favour of pressing engagements or younger siblings. Allowing the child to choose the activity gives them a strong message that this is their time. Indeed, special time together can be used as a reward for co-operative behaviour.

3. **Remember the power of praise.**
    The issue of praise and rewards is dealt with in more detail later in this chapter. It cannot be overemphasised, however, that praising your child increases the chances that they will repeat that behaviour. Be specific in your praise: "That is a beautiful picture you drew for me" is much better than "You are a great girl". Parents should be on the lookout for those times when the child is happily engaged on their own and it is tempting to say, "I will leave well enough alone". Don't. Go in there and let them know how pleased you are.

4. **Set limits.**
    With the increasing pressures on families from outside influences, it is essential that rules are established and adhered to. It is quite acceptable to involve the children in putting together household rules. Indeed, it is desirable. If they are part of the conception of the rules, they are more likely to abide by them. Parents will be amazed at how reasonable children can be once they feel involved. Now more than ever before, children need to have limits set on what is or is not acceptable. Included in the rules must be the consequences of flouting household rules.

5. **Remain calm. Avoid letting your child see you angry in times of stress.**

   This may be a tall order, so it is best to have contingency plans ahead of the inevitable. Children will often drive you beyond your level of tolerance. That is part of family life. If a child knows what buttons to push to make their parents angry, they will do so any time they crave attention. In these circumstances, it is best to leave the room, count to ten, practise deep breathing, ask a neighbour to watch the children while you go for a walk or whatever it takes to alleviate your stress at these times. One method of relieving stress is the practice of yoga. Parents might consider taking a course if they have not already done so in order to maintain a sense of balance amid the chaos.

6. **Be consistent.**

   Another button children seem to be adept at finding is the one for guilt. There are times when it might seem easier and less problematic for parents to acquiesce to the child's unreasonable request. However, if parents compromise the standards already set, these are more likely to be ignored repeatedly by the child. It is preferable to endure a tantrum or be temporarily hated rather than be held hostage to fortune.

7. **Avoid the drive for perfection.**

   Neither the parent nor the child is perfect. The pursuit of perfection is a fruitless exercise. Strive for excellence rather than waste time seeking perfection. Sometimes parents set unattainable standards for themselves and their children. A certain amount of competitiveness is evident among parents. The age at which a child walked, talked or was toilet-trained is set down as a marker of good parenting in some circles. A sense of failure can overcome the parents whose child is not at least two months ahead of what the current parenting manual said. This is unproductive. Children reach milestones when they are ready. Some parents are reluctant to take their child to the supermarket in case they have a tantrum in public. Parents will be relieved to know that the reaction of most other parents upon witnessing a child's tantrum is "Thank God it is not mine today".

8. **View bad behaviour as a time to learn.**

   It can be demoralising for parents who are doing their best but feel as if they are getting nowhere when their child misbehaves. The way to break out of this cycle is to step back and try to identify where the problem may have started. Was the child hungry? Tired? It should be noted here that lack of sleep is significantly related to behaviour problems with children. Regardless of the problem encountered, parents should consider what they would do differently if similar circumstances were to arise. Plans should be put in place to avoid a repeat.

9. **Spend time at the child's level.**

   This advice is meant to be taken literally. When talking to a child, parents should get to the same eye level. This will make communication much easier. Parents should be prepared to get down on the floor, lie on the bed, sit beside the child, dance with them or whatever brings them to the child's level. When talking with the child, use simple language: short words and short sentences will make communication much more effective.

10. **Ignore minor misbehaviour.**

    This is one of the most effective parenting strategies parents can adopt but it is not easily put into practice. It is most effective when carried out in an environment where co-operative behaviour is recognised. Ignoring minor misbehaviour sends a very strong message to the child and increases the chances that they will not want to repeat the behaviour. For example, if the child is seeking your attention by using foul language, the best course of action is to ignore rather than reprimand them. If there is a sibling present who is not using bad language, engage with that child. This sends an even stronger message to the offending child.

11. **Take small steps.**

    Parents who are having a difficult time with their child should not try to deal with all aspects of the problem at the same time. Whether the task is toilet-training a toddler who must accomplish this skill prior to going to pre-school or grappling with the nightly battle royal over homework, it is best to break the task down into small steps. All parenting tasks should be approached in a step-by-step fashion.

12. **Keep the communication lines open.**

    This is a priority in all relationships but particularly between parents and children. Children will be more likely to tell parents about problems they are encountering (such as school bullying) if they feel comfortable talking with their parents. Keeping the communication lines open also requires honesty from the parents. For example, if a parent is feeling sad about an issue, it is acceptable to let the child know. Children are naturally intuitive and may worry unduly in the absence of real discussion. So effective communication requires straight talking in both directions. Obviously, this needs to be at a level that the child will understand.

13. **Consistency among carers is the key to success.**

    The most important area for consistency is between spouses. Children will inevitably ask the other parent in the event that one will not acquiesce to a request. Spouses must be supportive of each other and consistent in their approach to parenting. If there is confusion or disagreement about how to apply the rules, it must be sorted out after the children have gone to bed. Even when both parents follow a consistent line, extended family can unwittingly sabotage the best-laid plans. At a minimum, aim for rules to be followed when the relatives are in your home. In their homes, application of rules should be discussed and agreed in advance.

14. **Plan ahead.**

    It is possible to prevent most problems through good planning. Parents should make a habit of planning at least a week in advance. Planning ahead also means involving the children in those plans and keeping them informed about what is upcoming. Problems arise when children do not know what is going on or when they feel left out of something that is going to affect them.

15. **Less is more.**

    Stop trying so hard. It is useful to step back from the parenting grind and not be available at all times. Children need to learn that the umbilical cord was cut at some point along the way. They need to understand that you are not a valeting service and that they can do without you sometimes. In this way, you will avoid being taken for granted.

16. **Create a positive culture in the home.**

    If parents compared the amount of time spent arguing, correcting or giving out in the home with the amount of time spent praising, complimenting, chatting or laughing with their children, the former would probably predominate. Aim to create an environment in the home in which positive exchanges predominate.

17. **Be authoritative not authoritarian.**

    It is important to maintain the boundary between parent and child, but not to the extent that the child feels distanced from the parent. Too much regulation is not healthy. If a child does not feel that they are being listened to or cannot make a meaningful contribution to family matters, they may become more inhibited. Run a democracy, not a military base camp.

18. **Model the behaviours you are looking for in your child.**

    A parent actually said to me once, "I don't know where the f***in' hell he's getting all that f***in' bad language from". The old adage of "do what I say and not what I do" does not hold any credibility. Children are much more likely to copy their parents. It is a sad fact that children whose parents smoke are five times more likely to smoke in adulthood. Parents are the primary role models for children.

19. **Get physical.**

    It is partly cultural and partly because we do not fully appreciate the benefits, but showing affection is an extremely important part of the parent–child relationship. And we do not do it nearly enough. If it does not come naturally to a parent, the advice is to learn how. For example, if you are not already doing it, a good start would be to commit to hugging your child at least three times every day for the next two weeks and observe the results.

20. **Believe in yourself.**
With all the conflicts, dilemmas, confusing advice and chaos which they encounter on a daily basis, parents may come to doubt their ability to raise their children. They should never lose sight of the fact that they are the experts about their own children. Parents know more about their children than anyone else and, while they listen to the advice and recognise the limitations of their circumstances, they should always do what they believe to be right for their children.

EFFECTIVE USE OF REWARDS

As mentioned earlier in this chapter, praise is a tremendous tool of effective parenting and is instrumental in building a child's self-esteem and confidence. In this section, we will examine how other types of rewards can be used effectively. How a parent distributes rewards is the cornerstone of positive child management. The principle is not much different to that which governs the business world, but the application of it certainly is. Essentially, when we provide a reward it increases the likelihood that the person will repeat the behaviour for which they received the reward. A personal example of how this principle works is how I choose my aftershave. I have a variety of them, picked up on my occasional trips through airport duty-free shops. If one of my female colleagues compliments me on my aftershave, it is not difficult to guess which one I will wear the following day. Similarly, people often favour a particular item of clothing because they have been complimented on it at different times. Children are no different.

They are much more likely to repeat a behaviour for which they have received praise or recognition. The outcome of a well-chosen reward is motivation.

Parents often confuse rewards with bribery. It is important to note that rewards are not bribes. Bribes involve paying someone off to do something wrong. A reward is a recognition for something done well. This is a subtle but necessary distinction. Giving a child sweets to quieten a tantrum is bribery; giving a child sweets because they shared their toys with their siblings is reward. The point here is not necessarily to increase the amount of rewards, but to be more selective about when rewards are provided. A good time to provide a reward is when a child has done something well, when the child is sharing or when doing something which parents approve of and want to encourage. The wrong time to provide a reward is when the child is cranky, uncooperative or rude. Finally, the most rewarding entity of all is the parent. Parents often do not realise what a rewarding entity they are for their children. Positive time spent with a parent is the most enjoyable and rewarding experience a child can have. There are different types of rewards that parents should consider using throughout each day. We can break them down into four categories: social rewards, activity rewards, material rewards and behaviour charts.

Social Rewards

These are the most powerful rewards of all and it is reasonable to suggest that we do not use these type of rewards nearly enough. As with many of the principles outlined in the book, these do not apply exclusively to children. Adults enjoy them just as much. The benefits of social rewards are many: they are cheap; all children like them; they can be given immediately; children never get tired of them; and they are readily available. Parents should aim to accompany praise with a hug or some type of physical contact. Here are some examples of social rewards:

✓ Hugs and kisses	✓ Smiles
✓ Praise	✓ Tickles
✓ Talking to the child	✓ Holding the child
✓ Telling others about the child's accomplishments	✓ Pat on the back

Activity Rewards

Parents and children often assume that the children have automatic rights to access many of the activities around the house. The television, video recorder, computer, bicycle, toy chest or roller blades are examples of activities which should be considered as "rewards" to be earned only following the completion of a task such as homework. This reality is often overlooked by parents in this era of children's rights without reference to responsibilities. There is an endless list of activities which can be used as rewards not only to motivate children but to create opportunities to develop the parent–child relationship. As my current favourite fridge magnet states: "The best things in life are not things".

✓ Trip to the park	✓ Feeding a pet
✓ Bedtime stories	✓ Eating out
✓ Being lifted into the air	✓ Planning the day's activities
✓ Taking a photograph	✓ Longer time in the bath
✓ Talking into a tape recorder	✓ Playing in a sandbox
✓ Helping out	✓ Playing outside
✓ Riding a bicycle	✓ Piggy back

✓ Bouncing on the bed	✓ Sitting on parent's lap
✓ Trip to the zoo	✓ Sitting on Dad's shoulders
✓ Helping to hold the baby	✓ Setting the table
✓ Baking	✓ Listening to favourite tape
✓ Freedom from chores	✓ Phoning grandparents
✓ Time in parents' bed	✓ Planning a meal
✓ Staying up late	✓ Displaying schoolwork on the fridge
✓ Dressing up in adult's clothes	✓ Blowing bubbles
✓ Camping in the back garden	✓ Gardening
✓ Playing with a magnet	✓ Playing on a swing

The list is endless. Not all these activities may apply to individual situations, but there will be others that can be considered as a potential reward.

Material Rewards

These are the most obvious rewards but they are not necessarily the most effective. If a child receives material rewards too regularly, they will cease to have either an interest or motivating value. Reserve special treats only for special occasions. Parents should not rely on material rewards to make up for what they might perceive they are not providing in other aspects of family life. There is no replacement for time spent with the children. Too much material indulgence will damage the child. As over-indulged children develop and move into the teenage years, it may be harder for them to be gratified by material goods. This is often when drugs and alcohol enter the fray. Examples of material rewards that should be used sparingly are:

✓ Toys	✓ Computer games
✓ Sweets and chocolate	✓ Pets
✓ New clothes	✓ CDs
✓ Favourite food	✓ Magazines

Behaviour Charts

There has been much discussion in parenting circles about the appropriateness of using behaviour charts (otherwise known as star charts or incentive schemes). Some people complain that they are too mechanical and degrading. They also feel that they will teach a child to want a reward every time something is done properly. My own position is that behaviour charts actually mirror real life. If we do something well or practise sufficiently hard, the rewards will come. If we do not put in the effort, not much will happen in return. This is surely a valuable lesson for any child to learn.

Children are in many different situations every day for which they do not expect or receive rewards, such as when playing with friends. The behaviour chart does not dominate the child's life. It is usually recommended in an area where the family might be encountering some problems, such as completing homework or carrying out simple household chores. It is not the case that it prompts the child to expect rewards every time something is done well. If this happens, parents should review how they are using the chart. In general, the chart is a very useful tool for parents and has many advantages over other types of rewards.

First, a chart is very simple to operate. Children as young as three years, and even younger, can understand the concept of a token being given following co-operative behaviour.

Second, a chart also provides a very tangible record of your child's good behaviour. At all times, parents should aim to create a positive culture in the home, where good behaviour is recognised and bad behaviour ignored. The chart assists in creating that type of environment. It is a visible record of the child's progress which can be shown to Mammy or Daddy when they come home from work. It also prompts any visitors to the home to comment.

Third, the chart means that parents do not feel compelled to provide material rewards on an ongoing basis. These can be reserved for when the goal or objective has been reached.

Another benefit is that every time a child earns a sticker, star or credit, it actually prompts the parent to notice the good behaviour and praise the child. Parents who have used behaviour charts often report that the child was not necessarily interested in the ultimate reward, but particularly enjoyed the operation of the chart with all the positive interactions it entailed. When a behaviour chart is in operation, it prompts parents to be on the lookout for good behaviour rather than being overwhelmed by the child's antisocial activities. Here are the steps involved in setting up a behaviour chart that works:

1. Make sure you have all the necessary materials ready for the chart such as tokens, sheets, stickers or whatever you will be using.
2. Have a chat with your child about what is involved in the chart and why you are starting it. For example, "This chart is going to help you have good manners at the table".
3. Describe how the chart works. Give a demonstration if necessary.
4. Enlist the child's assistance in designing the chart. There is no limit on how creative you can be.
5. Explain how the child will earn a token if there is co-operation for a specified period of time. (This should be quite short in the initial stages until the child is used to the system.)

6. Describe that there is a reward after the child has earned X amount of tokens.
7. Ask the child to repeat the rules for the star chart.
8. Explain that no rewards will be given if the child does not earn the tokens.
9. Use praise when giving the child a token.
10. Make sure to provide the reward as soon as the required number of tokens has been earned.

Figure 4.1: **Example of Behaviour Chart for Younger Children**

Figure 4.2: **Example of Incentive Scheme for Teenagers**

Checklist of Completed Chores*							
Chore	Mon.	Tues.	Wed.	Thurs.	Fri.	Sat.	Sun.

* Pocket money to be determined by number of chores completed.

Behaviour charts are not always constructed in a way that is beneficial to the user. If the chart is not working, it is time to go back to the drawing board rather than throw in the towel. There are good and bad examples of behaviour charts from which we can learn.

This may come as a surprise to many people, but the most effective star chart of which I am aware is the Superquinn Superclub. The principles involved are no different to the operation of a sticker chart to encourage a child to brush their teeth. Superquinn want people to shop in their establishment. Those who do, earn points: if they shop early in the week, they get double points; if they buy products on special offer, they double up on points again; if they report an item out of stock or broken they are rewarded with more points; and when they collect so many points they can exchange them for an item from the Superquinn catalogue. So, on the basis of the Superquinn star system, the day a person shops and the products a person buys are strongly influenced by the store. Customers even do quality control without realising it! It is a simple but very effective star chart. However, the really motivating aspect of the Superclub is the range of items that can be earned through the catalogue. Contrast this with incentive schemes in other supermarkets that only offer a single item. Which is more motivating? When parents do get around to setting up a chart with their child, they should consider compiling a small catalogue of rewards to be earned. This will undoubtedly increase the child's motivation.

Parents often ask when they should stop using star charts. It is not uncommon for the child to want to keep them long after the problem behaviour is sorted out. It is certainly not necessary to persist with behaviour charts indefinitely. Time usually erodes their significance for the child and the behaviour itself becomes rewarding. The rule of thumb is to use the chart as long as it is working.

Finally, it should be noted that behaviour charts are applicable to all ages. Depending on the age of the child, the format will change. But, as demonstrated with the Superquinn example, the principle is universal.

CHAPTER 5

Things We Cannot Change

The complexities of what causes your child to behave in a certain way are many and varied. While the bulk of this book deals with the aspects of your child's environment over which you can have a positive influence, this section covers the aspects that cannot be changed. Parents often remark on the different personalities of their children. It is probably stating the obvious to mention that no two children are the same, even within the same family. These differences come about from a whole range of interactions between environmental factors and natural phenomena. Scientists disagree about the extent of the influence of each. This is known as the nature–nurture debate. Without attempting to enter into such rarefied scientific argument, outlined below are some of the natural phenomena that influence behaviour but that cannot be changed. It is useful for parents to understand where these differences come from before they set out to create a positive parenting environment.

FAMILY CONSTELLATION

There is no doubt that the child's place in the family birth order has a significant influence on subsequent development. Every child has a different perspective on the family by virtue of their position within it.

- First-born children have a very privileged and unique position in the family. Whole books have been written on the personality types of first-borns. The first-born receives considerably more attention than subsequent children. These children are more likely to adopt the characteristics and values of their parents than are subsequent siblings. They tend to be more strongly motivated towards achievement, more affiliative and conformist than their brothers and sisters. Compared to their siblings, first-borns tend to be more responsible, less aggressive and more intellectually curious. When the second child arrives they are suddenly dethroned. First-borns may want to maintain their status and will strive to protect this favoured position. They might lose interest in activities in which they cannot maintain supremacy. This is why first and second-born children usually excel at very different activities. Sometimes the first-born can become discouraged if not winning out over subsequent siblings and may become "best" at exhibiting uncooperative behaviour.

- Second-born and subsequent children will experience someone who is always ahead of them. They may feel inadequate, because the older child can do things that they are unable to do. Or they may feel they have to catch up by striving to become what the older child is not. Second-born children are more likely to be realistic in self-evaluations and less cautious in behaviour – for example, being more likely to participate in extreme sports. By virtue of their place in the family, they must consider the needs and wishes of others, which builds important social skills. These social skills generalise to life outside the home. As a result, second-borns are more likely to have more success in interacting with peers, which leads to greater popularity.

- Middle children can often feel squeezed out, deprived of the rights and privileges of those on either side. A belief may develop that life is unfair. Alternatively, they may decide to overcome the disadvantages of being in the middle and strive to be better than any of the other siblings.

- Youngest children are often seen as the "babies" of the family, which can lead to a certain ineptitude on their part. They may be more manipulative than their older siblings. Parents are more likely to be flexible regarding household rules with the youngest child. Having been around the block a few times by this stage, parents may not be as cautious as they were with the older children.

- Only-children experience their formative years among people who are bigger and more capable, and can thereby develop a style that ensures them a place among adults. They may become verbal and charming or, if it suits their purpose, shy and helpless. Only-children have a tendency to expect to have their own way much of the time.

The Sex of the Older/Younger Sibling

The sex of the older/younger sibling is another significant factor in moulding personality. When there are a number of boys in the family the younger children are more likely to have "masculine" traits. Girls with older brothers are more likely to be able to hold their own among boys than girls with older sisters. And boys with older sisters tend to be less aggressive and less daring than boys with older brothers.

Personality Types

Children are born with particular personality traits that have a major influence on their subsequent development. These traits are major contributors towards moulding the personality of an individual throughout their life. Outlined below are some of the personality traits that have been noted in infants. Consider your child's personality as you read through each trait.

Level of Activity
Some children are naturally much more active than others.

Regularity
In the early stages, regularity is evident through sleeping, feeding and changing patterns. Some parents report no difficulties, while others can have notable problems around routine care. This trait of regularity – or irregularity – can remain well into the adult years.

Response to New Situations or Events
Individual children respond in different ways to new situations or events. For example, parents sometimes wonder why one child is frightened by Santa Claus while the other jumps up on his knee and will list all gift requirements without prompting. Put it down to personality!

Adaptability to Change in Routine
Some children can cope with changes in routine while others cannot. A child's inability to cope with change may sometimes be attributed to bad behaviour. Perhaps it could be interpreted instead as a trait in the child's personality.

Sensitivity to the Environment
Some children are extremely sensitive to their environment. For example, some children may tolerate a noisy environment much more easily than others.

Intensity of the Response

Some children may scream the house down over the most minor incident. Others will have a more placid demeanour. We can all readily identify friends and colleagues who fall into either category of responsiveness to their environment.

Cheerfulness

Parents frequently wonder why one baby can be so happy and the next one never seems to stop crying. This is not unusual – consider any gathering of people to remind yourself of the range of differing personality types.

Concentration Span

From observing the mobile over the bed for hours as a baby, to studying for the Leaving Certificate as a worried teen, this aspect of personality appears to be consistent over time.

Intensity of Concentration

The final trait in our list identifies a characteristic that could also be called freedom from distractibility. Babies can vary in their ability to maintain a focus. This is obviously a trait which, if present, is a significant asset throughout one's life.

There are probably as many theories of personality as there are personalities. What is important to note here is that children are born with certain attributes that will stay with them for life.

CHAPTER 6

Self-Esteem, Bullying and Friends

SELF-ESTEEM

Perhaps more than any other aspect of parenting advice, self-esteem has featured most prominently in the literature of the past ten years. In my opinion, too much attention has been given to this topic. This is particularly the case today, when children have more material goods than ever before and their happiness seems to be dependent on whether they have the most recently marketed item. Many parents cannot bear the thought that their child might feel inferior to other children if they do not own the latest must-have item. Ensuring a child is in possession of the most recent fad item in no way preserves or boosts their self-esteem. On the contrary, it reinforces their dependence on peer-group influence for approval and status. There is no doubt that there are many innovative and useful items on the market which are of benefit to the child, but parents must fight this slavery to faddism which has spiralled out of control with the blinding range of media to which children are now exposed. Products are being marketed from every angle. Children have to learn that their status does not depend on the possession of newly acquired toys.

There are three core questions to consider in relation to a child's self-esteem:

1.   Is my child happy?
2.   Does my child have friends?
3.   Is my child actively involved in some type of sports and/or hobbies?

If the answer to all three of these questions is "Yes", there is very little to worry about in the area of self-esteem.

If the answer to any of these questions is "No", parents may need to return to the principles outlined in Chapter 5. Building self-esteem need not be a complex issue. The following checklist is useful for parents to review the current status of their child's progress.

- Am I spending enough time with my child?
- Am I giving my child enough praise?
- Does my child have sufficient opportunity to have new experiences?
- Is there a positive culture in my home?
- Does my child experience success from time to time?
- Do I avoid unnecessary criticism of my child?
- Have I set realistic goals for my child?
- Am I patient with my child?
- Am I a good role model for my child?
- Are my child and I capable of having fun together?
- Am I boosting my child's strengths?
- Do I teach my child to be positive and think positively about themselves?
- Do I facilitate my child to achieve at their own level?

If the answer is "No" to any of the above questions, the necessary steps should be self-evident. On the other hand, if it is evident that the child is enjoying all these aspects to a reasonable level and still seems out of sorts, it may well be that there are issues outside of the home to be addressed, for example problems in school.

Bullying

Bullying is one of the most destructive experiences a child can encounter and must be taken very seriously. If anything can damage a child's self-esteem, bullying can. Children are generally very resilient and can adapt to most situations. Bullying can hurt even the most resilient child. It must be dealt with head-on. Parents should not tolerate bullying at any level. This is the case whether your child is being bullied or is the bully. It should be noted that children from wealthy families can fall into either category depending on individual temperament. Coming from a family of considerable means can cause a child to be targeted by a bully. Conversely, a child who is spoiled has potential to turn into a bully themselves.

Bullies are cowards and generally have lower IQ scores than normal. They also have low self-esteem. These children usually have emotional, behavioural or learning deficits. Family factors have also been identified, including a negative attitude between parent and child, overly punitive discipline, inconsistent or lax control and a household where physical aggression is seen as socially acceptable.

Bullying has been noted to be twice as common in primary schools as in secondary schools. Victims tend to have notable physical characteristics, such as wearing glasses or being overweight, and are likely to be passive or timid. Whatever the reason why some children bully, it should not be tolerated. Thankfully, many schools have been very proactive in addressing the problem of bullying and have programmes in place to prevent it. However, bullying remains an issue in some schools. Any of the following indicators could be signs that your child is being bullied:

- Child previously enthusiastic about school loses interest
- Requests to be driven to and from school
- Damage to personal property
- Child returns home from school in a bad mood but refuses to say why
- Unexplained changes in mood
- Frequent minor illnesses
- An increase in requests for money
- Unexplained cuts or bruises
- Child threatening suicide (this must be taken seriously).

If parents suspect their child is being bullied, they should speak to the child's teacher about it. It should be noted that if the child is demonstrating some of these behaviours, it does not automatically mean they are being bullied. These behaviours simply signal that further investigation is warranted.

There are a number of steps a parent can take if it is known that the child is being bullied. Parents must take steps to address the problem as quickly as possible:

- Encourage the child to talk about the problem. The child may fear that the bullying will get worse if it is discovered that parents are involved. Parents should reassure the child that this will not happen. For younger children, it is important that they attend a playschool that encourages children to report if someone is hitting. "Telling teacher" is OK in a well-run pre-school.
- Stay calm. If parents get too annoyed the child may go back into their shell.
- Boost the child's confidence with plenty of praise.

- Teach the child assertiveness skills.
- Role-play situations with the child in dealing with situations when confronted by a bully.
- Encourage the child to ignore the bully and to make new friends.
- Encourage the child to develop new activities that will boost confidence. Scouts, drama, music, dancing, sports or martial arts are all areas that could be just the change the child will benefit from.
- If the bullying is happening at school the parent must meet the teacher to come up with a plan to tackle the problem. If the problem remains, parents should contact the school principal.

It would be unusual if this were not sufficient to sort out the situation. However, if the problem persists, parents should consider moving the child from the school. It is not worth persisting with the issue indefinitely. There are thousands of adults whose most vivid memory of their time in school is the dark days of being bullied. Alternatively, parents could choose to keep the child at home and write to the Department of Education about the problem. The Department may advise on a course of action, but whatever course of action is chosen, parents must be decisive.

Once they become aware of the problem, parents of a bully must take action before the child's behaviour deteriorates further. A child who bullies usually has problems well beyond the antisocial behaviour being demonstrated towards peers. If their child is a bully, parents should consider the following:

- Confront the child about the problem.
- Have the child acknowledge the wrongdoing of the actions.

- Set out rules and consequences for any further instances of bullying behaviour.
- Work on the child's self-esteem, as it must be low if this behaviour is being demonstrated.
- Try to have the child change the peer group which may be encouraging them in this direction.
- Role-play with the child what it must be like for the victim
- Set new goals for the child.
- Make it clear that this behaviour will not be tolerated (criticise the behaviour and not the child).
- Seek professional help if concerns remain.

In general, always check if the child's playschool or school has a policy on bullying. The child needs to be confident about approaching the teacher in the event that bullying is occurring. The child also needs to feel confident about telling their parents.

FRIENDS

Much as parents might like to, they cannot pick their child's friends. However, if a parent has good communication with the child, it is possible to give them some advice. But there is no guarantee that the advice will stick. Below are a number of pointers which should assist parents to encourage their child in the right direction:

1. Do not pick the child's friends but be enthusiastic about positive friendships.
2. Encourage the child to try different activities, clubs or hobbies.
3. Be aware that some children have many friends while others choose to have only a few. Either situation is fine as long as

the child is happy. When the child has no friends and is miserable, parents can take a more active role in assisting the making of friends.

4. Invite children over to the family home and help the children to have fun.

5. Avoid criticism of the child's friends.

6. Encourage the child to be pleasant company. The child may not realise it, but nobody is attracted to someone with a long face who has nothing nice to say.

7. Be aware that spoiled children can have great difficulty making friends.

8. Role-play good social skills with the child if making friends does not come naturally. Work on things such as pleasant facial expression, taking an interest in other people's activities and being a good listener.

9. Encourage the child to have friends in a number of different areas. For example, there can be one set of friends at swimming and a different group of friends in the neighbourhood.

10. Monitor friends who may be taking advantage of the child, particularly if the child is of a generous nature. Parents may find that their child is losing out in the exchange of toys with children who have more forceful personalities. Direct intervention may be called for in these situations.

CHAPTER 7

The Teenage Years

Parents who are currently facing the challenges of raising a teenager may well identify with the remarks of one commentator who described puberty as a two-year mental illness. Many parents ask themselves, "What happened to that lovely, friendly, innocent child I had six months ago?" Whatever the perspective on teenage years, there is no disputing that it is a time of change. Indeed, it is the most turbulent period of our lifespan, the transition from childhood to adulthood, from dependence to independence, from parents to peer group, from innocence to reality. Many individuals glide through puberty without a hitch. But there is a greater likelihood that if problems are going to emerge they will do so at this time.

There is a vulnerability about the teenage years, a naiveté which is depicted by Harry Enfield's television character, Kevin the Teenager. Kevin probably encapsulates the worst characteristics of the teenage stereotype. He is rambunctious, oppositional, spoiled, ungrateful, uncaring and rude to his parents. Not all teenagers match this stereotype, but I am sure that there are more parents who would identify with Kevin's parents than there are teenagers who would identify with Kevin.

The teen years are a time when the peer group takes on more prominence. Attitudes, fashions, activities and behaviour are determined by what peers are doing. It is ironic that as teenagers strive to be different, they all wear the same clothes. They are the group to whom the title "slaves to fashion" could best be applied.

The need to conform to the peer group is an expression of insecurity and a wish for acceptance. However, the satiation of this insecurity comes at a price – the well-recognised MTV culture has cornered the market in teenage rebellion. Unscrupulous marketers are fully aware of this insecurity and have the exploitation of it down to a fine art. Every pop star and famous footballer is a walking billboard. These marketing moguls are also aware that parents are more likely to spend their hard-earned cash on their teenager than on themselves. "Everyone else is allowed" could be the teenage anthem. Parents must be extremely careful in this era of plenty. If there is an inclination to spoil a child, it is in the teenage years that the fallout of allowing a child have too much will become evident.

This is a time when the teenager must learn to cope with the outside world and they will not always be able to depend on parents for survival. It must also be acknowledged that there is probably more pressure on teenagers today than ever before. Peer and media pressure to drink, take drugs, smoke and have sex before they are ready has never been so great. Teen magazines write about sexual matters such as oral sex, new sexual positions and physical attributes in a most irresponsible way. In addition, Leaving Certificate exam pressures are probably greater today than at any other time. Pressures to conform often do not take account of the lack of maturity of the teenager. This is a recipe for trouble. Parents need to be aware that this is a time of tremendous change for the teenager. They should not take things personally. Oppositional behaviour is often the teenager's effort at exploring the boundaries of what is acceptable and what is not. Sometimes this can be ugly, sometimes not. And in the middle of all this vulnerability, insecurity, discovery, moodiness and change they get spots! It is not fair.

A first step in assisting a teenager through the potentially bumpy ride of adolescence is to be aware of the changes that are actually taking place. These come under the headings of physical, emotional, social and sexual development.

PHYSICAL CHANGES

- Growth spurt.
- Development of sex glands: ovaries mature in girls; testicles mature in boys.
- Appearance of secondary sexual characteristics: breasts in girls; facial hair and voice breaking in boys. These can occur any time between the ages of 13 and 18.
- Acne is the inevitable outcome of all the activity in the glands. If severe, it is recommended to seek medical attention.

EMOTIONAL CHANGES

- The release of sex hormones around the body stimulate sexual feelings. Experimentation with sexuality is inevitable for some, while others may become frustrated as a result of their inhibitions.
- Impulsive behaviour is another common trait associated with adolescence. Moodiness and oppositional behaviour is to be expected; however, extremes of this behaviour call for professional help.
- Anxiety about growing up is evident at this stage. Some teenagers embrace their new-found freedoms, while others hang back and postpone the inevitable for as long as possible.

SOCIAL DEVELOPMENT

- This is particularly difficult for teenagers today owing to the mixed messages emanating from family, church, media and peers.
- There is a marked shift from seeking the support and security of parents to looking for the same from the peer group instead.
- The teenager must start contemplating the future with respect to career choice, third-level education and other markers of adulthood.
- The teenager must adapt to a new sense of self.
- The teenager will form philosophical and societal values. Idealism will be at its height.

SEXUAL DEVELOPMENT

- Interest in sex is greatly increased.
- Masturbation becomes the norm. Teenagers still worry about the myths which circulate around school yards and this can create feelings of guilt or anxiety. They need reassurance that it is perfectly normal.
- Experimentation with members of the opposite sex is common.
- Inner conflicts develop between, on the one hand, the desire for sexual contact and, on the other hand, fear of rejection, feelings of inadequacy, disapproval and concerns about pregnancy and sexually transmitted diseases.

COMMUNICATION

The changes outlined above are only a brief sketch of the myriad of changes that actually occur during the teenage years. Patience and understanding is called for but often difficult to give if the teenager is unresponsive and moody. Good communication is the key to a supportive relationship with your teenager. Talk to your children about everything: peer pressure to conform, drugs and alcohol and sexual development issues (STDs, AIDS, masturbation, contraception, pregnancy and dating are some of the more essential topics). Household rules should be routinely discussed. Some parents may find it difficult to talk about certain topics. It is critical that they overcome this reticence about potentially embarrassing topics. It might be easier to introduce the topic by prefacing it with a reference to how parents developed their own understanding of these issues during their teenage years. The more parents talk about these issues, the less embarrassing they become. It is important to keep in mind that, if parents are not talking to their teenagers, their attitudes and values will be formed by peers and the media.

- Do not assume the teenager knows as much as they pretend to know – this is most often bravado. Parents will find that teenagers will be listening to every word of advice while dismissing their words in the same breath.
- Parents should take an active interest in their teenager's activities.
- Respect areas of privacy. It is probably best to stay out of a teenager's bedroom. Naturally, if the bedroom is shared this will not be possible. But every effort should be made to allow a teenager some autonomy.
- Be a good listener. Try not to interrupt a teenager who is

talking. Show interest by attending to the person as they speak.

- Parents should clearly express their own values. They do not have to compromise their own core beliefs just because the teenager's peer group thinks differently.
- Have clearly stated rules on issues such as homework, pocket money, chores and curfews.
- Be flexible. Instead of imposing their own morals on their teenager, parents should help them to work out their own values.
- Avoid criticism. Teenagers are particularly sensitive to any form of criticism as they are feeling particularly vulnerable in the first place.
- Be loving and supportive while knowing that it may not always be reciprocated or appreciated.

Sometimes, however, good communication is not enough. Drugs and alcohol have a nasty lingering presence around all teenagers today. They are a constant source of worry for parents. Once again, awareness, vigilance and decisive action are necessary to curb this plague of the innocence of youth. It appears that the age at which teenagers begin to experiment with drugs and alcohol is becoming younger and younger. Teenagers engage in this self-destructive behaviour because of:

- Availability: parents need to be aware that drugs are widely available
- Peer pressure: copying adults
- Acting "big": despite all the warnings, the number of celebrities now smoking in the public eye is remarkable; the ban on overt advertising of tobacco has simply gone underground
- Boredom: teens who are not involved in sports or hobbies have

a much greater chance of being involved in antisocial behaviours
- Emotional problems that may be eased by drugs or alcohol.

Parents of teenagers should watch out for the following signs, which may indicate that their child is abusing drugs or alcohol:

- Loss of appetite.
- Uncharacteristic aggression or irritability.
- Sudden unexplained changes in mood.
- Frequent sullen, moody behaviour.
- Changes in sleep pattern.
- Loss of interest in friends, hobbies, sport or school work.
- Unusual stains, marks or smells on the body or clothes or around the house.
- Unusual behaviours such as selling belongings, stealing money or telling lies.

If parents know their teenager is engaging in these behaviours, they must take decisive action:

- Clearly prohibit all use of drugs. People who smoke are more likely to take drugs and drink alcohol. This must be spelled out to your teenager.
- Spell out the numerous dangers of drug-taking which may not be so obvious to the teenager.
- Find out exactly what drug is being taken and in what quantity.
- Try not to overreact as the problem may escalate in these circumstances. Be patient.
- Determine if the drug-taking was experimentation out of curiosity or a more long-term habit. Parents' response should be determined by the extent of its use.

- Inform the teenager that drug-taking and underage drinking are against the law.
- Keep the communication lines with the teenager open.
- Practice with the teenager how to say "no" to drugs and alcohol. Discuss with them situations in which they may be offered these illegal substances. Assist them in developing a strategy to refuse the temptation.
- Parents should seek professional help if they believe that their teenager has a chronic problem.
- Develop a clearly defined set of rules regarding co-operation and lack of co-operation around the use of drugs and alcohol.
- Encourage the teenager to participate in activities that are incompatible with drug and alcohol consumption such as sports, hobbies and clubs.
- Parents who are aware of a problem should work with their teenager's school to address it. Most schools should have a drugs-prevention programme in place and will be aware of the concerns of parents.

Finally, parenting teenagers can be just as rewarding as any other stage of the child's upbringing. It is a different time, but with patience and understanding of the rapidly changing world of a teenager, it need not be the trial so often portrayed in various quarters. Parents should:

- EXPECT increasing maturity, responsibility and independence.
- MAKE CLEAR what they approve of, disapprove of or merely tolerate.
- ACT THEIR AGE – teenagers will not be impressed by "trendy" parents.
- BE FIRM – striking a balance between applying reasonable standards and allowing the development of independence.

- BE SUPPORTIVE – by avoiding criticism of the teenager.
- BE CONCERNED but not overprotective.
- SET A GOOD EXAMPLE – actions speak louder than words.
- SEEK PROFESSIONAL ADVICE if a teenager is excessively or consistently depressed.
- REMEMBER – negative attitudes towards parents are often disguised ways of seeking adulthood, striving for independence or questioning values.

CHAPTER 8

Notes on Separation/Divorce/One-Parent Families

Statistics vary on the number of divorced or separated families in the general population, but estimates go as high as one-third of all families. Reasons for this are many. Certainly, in years past, a common practice in Ireland was for an estranged couple to stay together under one roof, for a variety of reasons: keeping up appearances, convenience, "for the sake of the children", staying stuck in a rut or intransigence. It may not be a popular view, but I believe that staying together in this type of tension-ridden arrangement can be even more damaging to the children of that family. Now, with the availability of divorce as well as the weakening of any stigma that previously attached to it, family separation is a more common phenomenon and one that has obvious effects on all involved.

When a couple splits up it is a hugely traumatic event for all parties involved, but the people likely to be most affected by the split are the children. There is no point in attempting to soften this reality. It is extremely distressing and unsettling for a child when parents split up. There are no winners. However, with greater awareness and understanding among the public at large, the impact of a divorce or separation on a child can be eased. It is important to keep in mind that children are very adaptable. With time, it is possible for them to adjust to the changed set of circumstances if arrangements are handled in a mature and sensitive manner by the parents. Divorce or separation need not cause long-term emotional damage if common sense and a consistent approach are applied. Parents should follow the guidelines below to assist in smoothing a very rough ride for all involved.

TELLING YOUR CHILD ABOUT THE SPLIT

- When informing children about an impending separation or divorce, both parents should tell all the children together. This should be done in as calm a manner as possible. It is probably the hardest thing a parent will ever have to do. However, if it becomes overly emotional, it will cause more worry and confusion for the child.

- In addition, the parents should jointly speak to each individual child to discuss that child's concerns.

- Parents should be as straightforward and honest as possible when informing the children about why they are separating. Children will have a much better chance of adapting to a new set of circumstances if they fully understand how those circumstances came about.

- Children should be reassured that both parents will continue to love them. Reinforce this commitment by setting up concrete times when visits will happen and make sure to honour this commitment.

- Reassure the children that they were in no way the cause of the divorce. Children will often blame themselves for the upheaval. Rather like when people blame themselves for what they did not do for the deceased following bereavement, children will blame themselves for creating the problem between their parents. They must understand that they had no part to play in causing the changed circumstances.

- Spouses should avoid fighting in front of the children, regardless of how acrimonious the split. The children should never be used by one parent to get at the other.

- It is important to reassure each child that they were born at a time when their parents loved one another.

- The child should understand that the love for them of both parents will not change. What has changed is that the parents no longer love each other.

ADJUSTING TO NEW FAMILY CIRCUMSTANCES

- Try to keep as much consistency as possible in the children's lives. If possible, try to maintain their living arrangements, clubs, friends, school or other domestic arrangements. This will help them to adjust to life without both parents.

- Encourage the child to talk about the new situation. Normalise it. Divorce or separation are a part of life and parents should not try to hide that fact. Answer the child's questions candidly. Naturally, parents will have to construct their responses to the child's level of understanding. These questions may come up at the most unexpected times.

Welcome them and give as much information as is reasonable.

- Separated couples should agree basic rules regarding parenting. No matter how acrimonious the split, it is critical that previously applied household routines and rules are maintained. Indeed, the time just after a separation is when children may test the limits of parental discipline. It is crucial to ensure that consistency in the application of these rules is maintained. Difficult as it may well be, discussing rules with an ex-partner on an occasional basis will pay dividends for the children.

- Separated couples should avoid criticising each other to their children. While a parent may have an intense dislike for their former partner, the child does not. Individual parents should not expect that the child will ever agree with their opinion of the other parent. Even if the child may hold the same point of view at a given time, as they grow older, they may develop a different perspective on why their parents split up and may grow to resent one parent for what they now judge to have been unfair criticism of the other.

- Recognise the difficulty of adjusting to changed circumstances for all parties. There is no point in trying to be a super parent to impress the child or give the impression that the break-up is not taking a toll. There will be days when it seems impossible to keep going. There will be days when the child may be impossible to deal with. On days like these, parents should reassure themselves that there will be better times ahead. Expect that the child will have similarly difficult days.

- The child needs reassurance that it is fine to be close to both parents. Do not let personal feelings interfere with this fundamental right of the child to love both parents.

• Make sure to inform the school of any new domestic circumstances. Some forward-thinking schools even have programmes to assist children whose parents are separated.

NORMALISING THE CHANGED CIRCUMSTANCES

• Grieving is a normal reaction to separation or divorce. At times the child may become angry towards their parents – this is part of the grieving process. If this period following a break-up is viewed as one of grief and renewal, it will be easier to have an understanding of some of the challenges facing parents.

• Both parents and children will eventually adjust to divorce or separation. Some experts estimate that it takes two years. The duration of this adjustment period varies from family to family. The main point is that adjusting to a divorce or separation takes time – and it should not be rushed.

• As the child grows older, parents are likely to be asked more detailed questions about the divorce. This is quite normal. Expect it and answer the questions as openly as possible. It will assist the child's ability to form their own relationships. Withholding information is much more damaging to the child.

• Children whose parents do not co-operate with each other around parenting practices have a higher chance of encountering problems than do children whose parents work together. However, if parents find themselves in situations where an ex-partner simply will not co-operate, they should concentrate on ensuring that they create a consistent approach to parenting in their own home. Parents may have to concede that they will only have influence over certain aspects of their child's life. The rest should be let go.

- Make time to talk to the child about living with only one parent. The inclination might be to "leave well enough alone", but this is inadvisable. Regardless of the demands on time, there is no more important use of it than talking with the child.

- Parents should not compete with an ex-partner for their child's loyalty or affection. If a child is forced into making choices between one parent and the other, they will become very confused. This type of scenario will exacerbate the difficulties the child is experiencing in the first place.

- Part of the consultation around parenting with an ex-partner should be about the distribution of treats and gifts. Non-custodial parents should avoid buying presents to make up for the time they are not spending with their child. If this is happening, keep in mind that its motivation is selfish and not in the interests of the child. What the child needs most when parents are separated is as consistent and stable an environment as possible.

- Preadolescents are a group who are particularly vulnerable when the parents split up. Be aware of this reality and be particularly sensitive to their reactions to the changed family circumstances. Consider professional help if it is felt that the adjustment is not going well.

- Stay healthy. Parents who separate go through an extremely traumatic time, as do their children. It is important that they look after themselves and allow for the fact that they have very deep feelings of hurt. They should talk to others and, if necessary, seek professional counselling.

THE NEW FAMILY CONFIGURATION

One possible result of separation or divorce is that new partners – and perhaps their children – often enter the frame. This can present difficulties for all involved. Children may fear that they will be displaced in their parent's affections. They may resent the new partner if they had harboured hopes that their parents might reunite. They may be resentful of having to share everything – from the parent's attention to living space – with the acquired "siblings". This is a situation that requires great sensitivity on the part of the adults involved, although there is a risk also of pandering to children's every whim to keep them "on side". Some points to note for parents or partners in a new family configuration include:

- Children in step-families or single-parent families have an increased risk of delinquent or antisocial behaviour. Peer-group influences are particularly strong for these children. Parents must make every effort to ensure that their children do not associate with undesirable peers, though this is not always possible.

- Although a parent and their new partner may view themselves collectively as "parents", children may not necessarily view the partner or step-parent in this context. It is more likely that the child will view the step-parent as a "friend" of the natural parent. This is not an easy issue to resolve. It must be must be done gradually and with great sensitivity.

- Step-parents should leave the major disciplining to the natural parent, particularly in the early stages of a new family arrangement. Inevitably, a child may test the limits with the step-parent. Over time, the optimal disciplining arrangements will emerge. Make sure that all parties agree on what should be done.

- Step-parents should not feel that they have to love the children in a new partnership. Similarly, the children may not form an automatic bond. The relationship between a step-parent and a step-child can develop any number of ways. Adaptability is key. Whatever the circumstances, try to figure out an arrangement that respects the child's feelings while ensuring that due consideration is given to the new partner.

- If possible, the non-custodial parent and the new partner should discuss household rules regarding the child.

Finally, as with any worthwhile approach to behaviour management, children can be assisted through a divorce or separation with good planning and a consistent approach in the application of that planning. It is important to acknowledge the pain involved in this process for all parties. It is also important to state that it is possible to survive the trauma and resume a normal and productive lifestyle for both parents and children when the situation is managed in a mature and open manner.

CHAPTER 9

Inheritance/Distribution of Wealth

"I want to give my children enough of an inheritance that they will feel like they can do anything, but not so much of an inheritance that they will not do anything."

WARREN BUFFETT

The fear that a child who inherits substantial wealth will either squander it or become an ineffective person because of it haunts many parents. One US survey has even put a figure on when a child's motivation might be negatively affected by substantial inheritance. It suggests that once the value of the inheritance exceeds the $3.4 million mark, difficulties may arise, although problems can also occur with much smaller accounts. Jesse O'Neill, author of the book *The Golden Ghetto*, has written about the dangers of an unhappy relationship with money.[1] She has stated that "A lot of have-nots look at money as freedom. But in truth that freedom can turn into sheer terror when there is no structure, no goal, no reason to get up in the morning." Jesse O'Neil found herself in similar circumstances and set up a website called "The Affluenza Project" to deal with exactly such problems.[2] Her observations probably echo what many parents fear could happen to their children.

1. *The Golden Ghetto: The Psychology of Affluence*, Jessie O'Neill, The Affluenza Project, 1997
2. www.affluenza.com

Equally, many parents fail to make sufficiently far-sighted plans, which results in a very ineffective transfer of wealth, unnecessary taxation and acrimonious arrangements.

The combination of ineffective planning of an estate and insufficient preparation of children for the duties that come with managing wealth are the twin influences that can result in wealth being destroyed. The long-term consequence is that wealth that could have been passed on for future generations to enjoy may simply not be available and it is left to future generations to restart the cycle of wealth creation.

The key to avoiding these pitfalls is for parents to plan for the successful transfer of wealth. This chapter describes in brief some techniques that, depending on circumstances, can be used to plan effectively for the transfer of wealth in an orderly and structured manner to maximise benefits to both parent and child. The ideas suggested are by no means a menu from which to pick and choose, as each needs to be executed professionally. Not all may be appropriate depending on circumstances. However, there are some core principles that do have a general application:

- **Start early.**
  The earlier you start planning the better. Ideally, you should start your planning before your child or children have reached their teens. However, there is always time to make appropriate arrangements, even if your children are already older.

- **Involve your whole family and educate the child.**
  When children are of an age to appreciate and understand, both parents should be involved in teaching them the benefits and responsibilities of money. If children's financial education begins earlier rather than later in life they will have a healthy relationship with money. A child will be at a distinct

disadvantage if they are suddenly thrust into the position of controlling a substantial inheritance without any experience of how to manage it. Some children may even feel that they do not have to work anymore and there are negative implications to this.

- **Understand that wealth can be destroyed.**
Too often, inherited wealth does not last beyond two or three generations. Naturally, this should not and does not have to be the case. Children who are educated about wealth and the responsibility that wealth entails will be able to make informed decisions about wealth preservation and growth.

- **The later the transfer of wealth happens the better.**
The collective wisdom on the transfer of wealth is that the later it occurs, the greater likelihood that the transfer will be smooth. Nowadays, many parents wait until their children are more mature before passing on the family fortune – one survey named thirty years of age as being the average. There is a genuine and valid fear among parents that younger children could easily lose the connection between work and reward. There is even a fear among some parents that if the transfer occurs too soon the child may end up controlling the parents' affairs. In order of priority, parents should address their own needs first, those of their children and heirs second and those of other beneficiaries (such as charities, donations etc.) third. It is important for parents to be aware of the downside of the transfer of wealth and to take action to avoid problems.

The passing on of wealth depends very much on the personality of the beneficiary. If a parent feels that the son or daughter is mature and capable of taking on the responsibilities that go with managing the family inheritance, then the options are easier to evaluate. It is when the parent is not so certain that the child is capable of taking on the responsibilities that go with wealth that a broader range of options should be considered. The following chart has been designed to assist parents to determine if their son or daughter is capable of inheriting in a responsible way.

Table 9.1: **Is my Child Ready to Inherit? Family Wealth Questionnaire**

1	Does my child show an interest in the well-being of other family members?	YES / NO
2	Is my child measured in how they spend money?	YES / NO
3	Does my child consider a range of options before buying a significant item?	YES / NO
4	Has my child an interest in helping those who are less fortunate?	YES / NO
5	Is my child able to avoid being exploited by unwelcome friends?	YES / NO
6	Is my child a confident individual with a strong sense of self?	YES / NO
7	Does my child have a range of healthy interests?	YES / NO
8	Does my child listen?	YES / NO
9	Does my child demonstrate maturity when required?	YES / NO
10	Is my child interested in world affairs?	YES / NO
11	Does my child have a commercial sense?	YES / NO
12	Does my child have common sense?	YES / NO
13	Does my child share my values?	YES / NO

14	Does my child take responsibility for their actions?	YES / NO
15	Does my child handle adversity well?	YES / NO

The greater number of "Yes" answers should increase parents' confidence in the child's ability to handle wealth in a responsible way. The more "No" answers registered suggest that parents need to put more thought into how wealth is imparted.

There are many options for the affluent parent when it comes to wealth transfer to their children. Outlined below are some of the more popular and tax-effective solutions. This list is by no means exhaustive and professional advice should be sought to identify the best planning match for your family's needs.

METHODS TO TRANSFER WEALTH AND RETAIN SOME DIRECTION OVER THE WEALTH

Family Partnerships/Family Limited Partnerships

In many cases, one of the reasons that parents are reluctant to transfer wealth to a child is the resulting lack of control and concern about gifting significant assets to their children. One solution can be found in a family partnership.

Essentially, a family partnership allows children to have beneficial ownership of assets but the parent retains control. The partnership agreement would not give the children any rights to manage the partnership property. This would rest with the parent as managing partner until the occurrence of a particular date or event, or quite simply when they are happy to hand over control.

It can make sense to purchase assets in the child's name under this arrangement, thereby allowing the asset to grow in the child's name without adding to Capital Acquisitions Tax (CAT) liabilities. CAT is the tax that arises on gifts/inheritances and is currently levied at 20 per cent.

Consideration can also be given to transferring assets into the partnership. For example, this may be ideal for cases where the child has an obvious interest and would like to build a career in the family business. Until such time as the child has proved themselves, control of family business assets will not be handed over.

Trusts

Simply put, a Trust involves giving legal ownership of assets to trustees, who manage them for the ultimate enjoyment of the beneficiaries. They can be of use to parents where, for example, there are concerns that a child may not be competent enough to manage wealth in an appropriate manner or the parent wants to protect assets for use and enjoyment by future generations.

A Trust deed sets out the intention of the person making the Trust and who it should benefit. It should also set out the terms and conditions governing the Trust and the powers given to the trustees.

In general, the terms of the Trust deed will provide either:

- That the trustees will hold the Trust property for the benefit of beneficiaries who have a fixed entitlement to the income or the capital of the Trust.

  For example, it may be the case that the parents never want the child to be in a position of control over the capital assets from which the family income is derived. Rather they simply want the child to be in a position to benefit from the income generated from these assets.

- That the trustees will hold the Trust property for a class of beneficiaries who have no fixed entitlement to either income or capital but merely a hope of benefiting at the trustees' discretion.

  A typical example of this would be where a testator has provided in their will that in the event of them dying while their children are young, their assets will be held on Discretionary Trust for the benefit of one or more of their children. The trustees can then exercise their discretion in deciding how, in what proportions and to which beneficiaries to distribute the funds, depending on circumstances at that time. Under this arrangement, the children of the testator have no fixed entitlement to benefit from the Trust funds but merely have a right to be favourably considered for a distribution.

The role of trustee is an onerous one and it is extremely important that whoever is going to take on the role is familiar with what it entails. They must have a full understanding of trustee duties and powers, and how these should be exercised. It is usually advisable to appoint a professional trustee to act alongside a lay trustee, to ensure that all obligations, legal or otherwise, are fulfilled.

Board of Management

A Board of Management could be used in the case of a family company. If there were an untimely death and some or all of the family members had an interest in the business, no one individual would have the opportunity to control the business without some recourse to the Board of Management. In this way, all interests are protected as well as the business itself from an otherwise potentially destructive party. For example, it may be the case that one individual is not interested in the advancement of the business but in using the business as a cash cow with the result that the business may not survive into the next generation.

Effectively this type of structure would involve a shareholders' agreement, which would also prohibit non-director family members being involved in the business unless all parties were in agreement. Typically, there would be a Board of Management that, for example, consisted of five members including two external independent individuals, perhaps a good business friend or a former auditor. The idea would be that the family members would benefit also from the experience and knowledge of the non-executive directors. There would be a clear management structure in place so that if any of the family members wanted to take a lesser role, then they would know that the business was properly run, their interests would be protected and they could simply continue to draw on their dividends/salary. There would also be a clear exit mechanism should they wish to realise the value of their shareholding.

METHODS TO HELP MITIGATE POTENTIAL TAX LIABILITIES ON THE TRANSFER OF WEALTH

Gifting Cash/Assets

Each child has a tax-free threshold (currently €456,438) of gifts/inheritances that can be taken before CAT will apply. This is a "once in a lifetime" limit in the sense that all gifts/inheritances taken since 5 December 1991 are aggregated for the purposes of ascertaining the remaining tax-free amount.

However, this aggregation date has been brought forward in prior years. For example, the aggregation date before 5 December 1991 was 2 December 1988. This supports an argument for at least transferring the child's tax-free threshold amount at an earlier rather than a later stage, given that the child's tax-free "slate" may well be "wiped clean" with prior gifts falling outside of the CAT net. Of course, depending on the child's age and maturity, suitable control structures should be put in place in tandem with making this lifetime gift.

It is important to bear this tax-free limit in mind when devising a will and splitting an inheritance amongst a number of children.

CAT Dwelling House Exemption

When carefully planned, the "Dwelling House" exemption can be used by parents as a means of setting up their children with a home of their own, the value of which falls outside of the CAT net.

Amongst the conditions to be fulfilled in order that this relief will apply are that the child must live in the house as their sole or main residence for a period of three years prior to the gift/inheritance and they cannot have an interest in another dwelling house at the time of the gift/inheritance. Furthermore, they must continue to live in the house for a period of six years after taking the gift/inheritance (subject to certain replacement rules) in order that no clawback would arise.

This relief may be very attractive in terms of planning for passing on the family home as there are no limits on the value of the residence it may apply to.

Same Event Credit

Where a parent makes a lifetime gift to a child, "Same Event Credit" relief operates to ensure that the tax implications of this gift are not more onerous than if this transfer occurred under the estate of the parent.

A gift is a deemed disposal for the purposes of Capital Gains Tax (CGT) and the parent is assessed to CGT as if they had disposed of the asset at open market value to a third party. A gift may also give rise to a liability to CAT for the recipient or the child in this case.

However, under "Same Event Credit", where both these taxes arise on the same event (the gift in this case), then the CGT arising may be used as a direct offset of the CAT liability. The value of the asset will appreciate in the child's name going forward as opposed to a CAT charge on the appreciated value of the asset at a later date. In addition, in the short term you have certainty about what the current rate of CAT is – that cannot be said about the CAT rate in the distant future.

The Use of Gross Roll-Up Funds

Gross Roll-Up (GRU) funds are unitised investment vehicles that can invest in shares, property, bonds or cash and are professionally managed by a fund manager.

Under current tax legislation, income and gains arising within the funds roll-up tax-free. Tax is only applied upon the occurrence of a "chargeable" event, which includes the disposal of units or the death of the last surviving investor. This tax is referred to as "exit tax" and is calculated at the standard rate of tax plus an additional 3 per cent (currently 23 per cent).

The main benefit of using these funds in terms of planning for wealth transfer is that the "exit tax" can be directly offset against the

CAT liability on inheritance of the remaining funds. This also ensures that the investor's estate is not at a disadvantage for the fact that they invested in GRU funds as opposed to a direct investment, for example, in property. Consider a direct investment: any CGT on gains up until the date of death is wiped out for tax purposes. If the exit tax credit did not exist, a double tax would arise upon death – exit tax on income and gains up until the date of death and CAT on the gross value of the units for the successor.

Business Reliefs

Tax legislation provides for the transfer of family businesses to the next generation without taxes being an onerous burden through the availability of various reliefs.

Under *Capital Gains Tax Retirement Relief* rules, a business may be disposed of to a child by way of gift or sale with no tax consequences for the person making the disposal once certain conditions are fulfilled. In the normal course of events, CGT would arise on this disposal. The current rate of CGT is 20 per cent. There is no limit on the value of the business to which this may apply. A business may include a sole trader, farmer or shareholding in a trading company owned by the individual. A blood niece or nephew who has worked in the business may also be treated as a child for the purposes of this relief, i.e. no CGT on the transfer of the business.

If a lifetime gift of the business is made to a child or if the business is passed on as part of the estate of the individual, then we need to consider the gift/inheritance tax implications of this. Normally this would be CAT at 20 per cent of the value of the business in excess of each child's CAT tax-free threshold (currently €456,438). However, under *CAT Business Property Relief* the value of the business assets may be reduced by 90 per cent before CAT is assessed. For example, shareholding in a family trading company valued at €4m is reduced to €400k when CAT is assessed. Ideally, the 10 per cent calculation will bring the value of the business within the child's tax-free threshold and no CAT will arise.

Both of these reliefs have particular conditions attaching and both apply automatically where the conditions of the relief are fulfilled. One important point to note, however, is that if the reliefs have been availed of then there will be a clawback if the child disposes of the business within six years. Another critical point is that the reliefs will not apply to investment assets.

The availability of these reliefs needs to be planned for, as they can easily be scuppered unintentionally. In relation to shareholding in a company, for example, neither relief will be available in the first instance, unless the company is deemed to be a trading company. The value of investment assets held within a company may have a negative impact on the "trading" status. It might, therefore, be timely to consider separating out trading assets from investment assets in order to secure these reliefs when the time comes to pass on the family business.

Section 72 Policies

A Section 72 policy should be used as the last tool in a good estate plan. Section 72 policies are simply life assurance policies that can be used to clear a CAT liability on death. The proceeds of the policy itself do not form part of the estate of the deceased for the purposes of calculating CAT once they are used to pay the tax on an inheritance taken within twelve months of the individual's death. Once the planning options to reduce the potential CAT liability on the estate have been thoroughly explored and exhausted, the remaining liability may be covered using this form of life assurance.

THE IMPORTANCE OF MAKING/UPDATING YOUR WILL

At the outset of planning for wealth transfer, it is recommended that you make a will and update it on a regular basis to allow for changing legislation and family circumstances. By having an up-to-date will in place, you can ensure that your estate will be wound up in accordance with your intentions (perhaps using some of the planning opportunities outlined above) with minimum delay and cost, avoiding confusion and dispute between family members. Importantly, your will affords you the opportunity to plan the tax-efficient transfer of your assets on death.

Finally, it is important that children understand what is happening financially. Money should not be a dirty word in a household of means. Children need to learn to become comfortable with this reality and develop a healthy attitude to money. So parents should be sure to talk about money to their children rather than viewing this as vulgar or unnecessary.

It is well documented that money causes people to react in the strangest of ways. The tabloid tales of so many lottery winners squandering their new-found wealth are evidence of that. Parents need to assess how they want their children to relate to money. It is impossible to guarantee a secure future, but by taking steps to create a healthy relationship with family wealth, it is eminently possible to get the balance right.

CHAPTER 10

The Family Business

M ost of us are familiar with the parable about the Prodigal Son. He cashed in his chips on the family wealth at an early stage in his development, blew it all on frivolous activities and eventually came back to his father with nothing. The father killed the fatted calf in celebration, leaving the sensible brother scratching his head about where he had got it all wrong. Most interpretations of the story centre around the father's unconditional love of all his children. But the big question that remained then, and I'm sure is asked by many parents today, is who should take over the family business. That was never answered in the parable. This chapter will attempt to address the relevant issues.

Parents understandably fear conflict within the family over inheritance. In the absence of a clearly laid-out plan, the chances of such a conflict are greatly enhanced. A number of different scenarios confront parents as they address the thorny issue of how to pass on the family wealth. But address it they must. Some of these scenarios are outlined below.

CHILDREN NOT INTERESTED IN CONTINUING THE FAMILY BUSINESS

One of the issues parents may face is what to do if no one in the family is interested in taking on the family business. Should it be sold while the parents are still alive? Should it be passed on to allow the children to decide whether to sell off the assets or maintain the business from a distance? Or should parents put pressure on their children to become actively involved in the family business or risk being written out of the will? Is the ownership of the business currently framed in a manner that could be against the child's interests if a co-director died?

Every family situation will differ. The answers to these questions will emerge when parents take a detailed look at the personalities involved and the practicalities of the situation. It is necessary for parents to be able to separate business interests from that of their role as parents in determining the best course of action. This is not an easy distinction to make and some of the main considerations will be addressed in this chapter.

SEVERAL FAMILY MEMBERS INVOLVED IN BUSINESS

Another possible scenario is when more than one of the children are involved in the family business. Inevitably, one or other of the children will have emerged as having greater leadership skills or as being more generally capable of running the business. This trend would have been very evident long before the issue of succession was a central issue. The inevitable jealousies must be recognised and dealt with through ongoing negotiation. Gender issues may play a part in considerations at this point. The tradition of the eldest male taking over the family business is no longer a foregone conclusion. When the moment of truth finally arrives, will tradition be left in the shadows and the most capable offspring be put in charge, regardless of gender? It is a daunting task for any parent to ensure family harmony is maintained through a projected transition period. Again, the issue of business concerns becomes entangled with those of the family. As far as possible, it is suggested to work always at keeping the two areas separate.

It should be clear by now that the issue of succession is one that should be planned for at as early a stage as possible. The more careful planning that is applied to this difficult issue, the greater likelihood of a successful transition. All parties should be clearly informed as to what they should expect. This should be an ongoing two-way process. If problems arise, it is preferable for the parents to be around so that they can do what is necesary to ensure that their wishes will be carried out.

INHERITANCE AND THE IRRESPONSIBLE CHILD

One possible situation which is as relevant today as it was in the biblical era described earlier is that of the irresponsible or aloof family member. What should a parent do when one of the children claims an equal share of the family business while doing little or nothing to contribute to its development? This may well be a situation where the separation of business and family interests is necessary. However, dealing with likely conflicts as early as possible and over time will reduce the chances of family dissolution in the event of the passing on of the business.

Perhaps an even greater worry for parents in such a predicament is the offspring who has not demonstrated a capacity to be responsible with money and who persists in claiming the share of family wealth to which there is a belief of entitlement. Parents should view such a scenario from the perspective of the past being the best predictor of what will happen in the future. That is, if one of their children has not demonstrated a capacity to be responsible with money in the past, it is more than likely that this will persist long after the parents can exert any influence over them. Parents may hope that the person will learn how to be responsible around privilege, but it is recommended that they plan for succession on the basis of practicality rather than sentiment.

USE OF CONTROL STRUCTURES

When it appears that no ready solution to the passing on of the family business can be arrived at, the prospect of setting up a suitable control structure becomes more real. For example, you may consider a trust structure, a family partnership or perhaps a board of management in the case of a family company. Each of these options requires careful planning and expert advice. Legal, financial, tax and even psychological input in the setting up of whatever type of control structure is chosen will ensure that the best solution is reached taking account of particular family circumstances to include parents' wishes while they are alive and also long after their passing. The essential point to remember is that by setting up a control structure, parents are ensuring their assets will be distributed in the manner they have chosen rather than the acrimony that invariably results from the absence of proper planning. We are all familiar with the horror stories of family divisions following in-fighting caused by the lack of a well-constructed estate plan.

The billionaire and philanthropist Warren Buffet chose an interesting means of distributing his vast fortune to his children. He made it clear that most of the family wealth would go to charities and that he would leave enough to his children to help them get started in life but he would not allow them to become lazy. While this may appear to be an extreme measure in order to ensure the psychological well-being of his children, it is a lesson of which most parents who are passing on significant wealth should take note. There is more than just financial security involved when wealth is being passed on to the next generation. It is not always a straightforward process. Succession of the family business requires planning which takes into account a range of different considerations and, ultimately, a certain amount of trust.

USE OF CO-DIRECTOR'S INSURANCE

There are also some practical steps that can be taken to protect one's interest where there are co-directors upon whose continued involvement the business may depend. Consider, for example, what could happen if your lifelong co-director and friend died suddenly and left their share of your business to an uninterested relative. The effect on your family's wealth could be devastating. Again some simple planning can be used to avoid such circumstances, such as taking out co-director or business partner assurance. Such policies are designed to release proceeds upon the illness or death of the insured such that this individual's interest in the business may be purchased from their next-of-kin/beneficiaries, thus avoiding the potential problems created by a disinterested or even an unintentionally destructive party being involved in the business.

CONCLUSION

Parents should try to step back from the domestic aspect of passing on wealth and develop an objective, pragmatic stance. It is a matter of recognising the personalities involved, projecting realistically about the future, taking professional advice, communicating effectively and ensuring settlements are made to everyone's satisfaction before parents are in a situation over which they have no influence. Ultimately, parents want their children to remain friends after they are gone. With good planning, this is a most attainable objective.

CHAPTER 11

And Finally...

Raising children is an onerous task for any parent. It is the one job for which no degree is required and yet it calls for so many skills on the part of the practitioner. Raising a child in the comforts of a wealthy environment presents a unique challenge. This book has identified the issues and made suggestions about how to avoid the associated pitfalls. While the world of business and the world of family life are very different, there are some universal principles which I believe can be applied across the board. The reader may find it useful to ponder how to apply these principles in the business of raising a family and also in the family business, two very separate domains.

1. **Effective Communication.**
   In the family context we have noted how important it is to communicate at the child's level, to learn how to listen to teens and to ensure open lines of communication with a spouse. A cornerstone of a successful business is effective communication both within an organisation and with partners and customers.

2. **Time.**
   Parents who are concerned about ensuring the best for their children should have realised by now that the optimal investment with the greatest return is time with the children. This is how values are instilled, futures are secured and self-

esteem is built up. How long would a business last without time devoted to it by its owner?

3. **Plan ahead.**
   The most effective parenting strategy is to put plans in place to anticipate upcoming events. Whether it is for a shopping trip, setting up household rules or deciding how to pass on family wealth, advance planning means that everyone feels in control. Again, one could and should apply the same logic when running a successful business.

4. **Recognise good behaviour.**
   Paying compliments and issuing praise are not attributes which come naturally to Irish people. However, learning how to recognise and acknowledge co-operative behaviour is a most powerful parenting strategy. It increases the likelihood of the child repeating the good behaviour. This is no different to an effective management strategy in the business world. A staff group or individual who receives recognition for a job well done will be much more productive than one who is ignored. The culture in the home or the workplace should be a positive one.

5. **Work first, then play.**
   While this may appear somewhat mechanical in the context of raising children, it is a principle which will pay dividends for parents and will benefit the child throughout their lifetime. Too often, parents get the order the other way around. How long would a business survive if it paid its employees before the work was done?

6. **Learn from mistakes.**
   When things go wrong between parents and their children

and stressors build up over time, parents tend to view themselves as failures. In their own eyes, the problems encountered simply confirm their presumed ineptitude. Parents are encouraged to take a different perspective when family matters appear to be getting out of hand. Aim to step back from situations and identify what aspect of it caused the problem in the first place. Was the child tired? Hungry? Bored? Make alternative plans for the next time that situation might arise in order to prevent the same problem from occurring. Anyone who enjoys a successful business enterprise could give the same piece of advice.

7. **Use rewards selectively.**
   This skill comes naturally to some parents and, indeed, to astute managers. It is the ability to observe closely and select the most appropriate time to recognise a job well done. For parents this translates into "Catch them being good". For the manager it translates into ensuring endeavour is recognised.

8. **Social awareness.**
   All children, but particularly privileged children, need to be aware that there are others who are less fortunate. Social conscience is a most desirable characteristic of any well-rounded individual. It can serve to remove the egocentric cloud which often stifles the potential of an over-indulged young person. A business which incorporates a similar perspective is also likely to have a staff group with more purpose and greater morale.

9. **Authoritative not authoritarian.**
   Children need to function with a clear set of family rules to guide them. Consistency in applying these rules is essential.

However, a home in which a child has few opportunities for autonomy and self-expression will create resentment and tension. Overly ambitious or anxious parents must learn to strike the right balance rather than feeling that they must control everything. Personal aspirations can sometimes cloud realistic expectations. Too much parental control will inevitably backfire. Similarly, a boss who is overly controlling in the business setting creates resentment and ultimately a drop in productivity.

10. **Model the behaviour you expect.**
    Children copy their parents. Employees' behaviour reflects that of management. The recommendation is to lead by example. A parent is a role model to the child in very much the same way as a manager is to employees. It would be unwise to underestimate the importance of one's own behaviour in influencing that of others.

Two very different worlds and both informed by very similar principles. Parents are encouraged to take the same practical view in planning for their children's well-being as they would in running a successful business.

This book has not attempted to inform parents how to love their children. Instead, it offers a framework on which parents can build an approach to parenting that works for them. This should, in turn, create countless opportunities for that love to be expressed. Very best wishes.